AF078991

Wild Dreams
ANIMAL ORACLE

Unleash Your Passionate Best!

KELLY SULLIVAN WALDEN
Artwork by Lisa Desimini

WILD DREAMS ANIMAL ORACLE
Unleash Your Passionate Best!

. . . .

Copyright © 2024 Kelly Sullivan Walden
Artwork Copyright © 2024 Lisa Desimini

All rights reserved. Other than for personal use, no part of these cards or this book may be reproduced in any way, in whole or part without the written consent of the copyright holder or publisher. These cards are intended for spiritual and emotional guidance only. They are not intended to replace medical assistance or treatment.

Published by Blue Angel Publishing®
80 Glen Tower Drive, Glen Waverley,
Victoria, Australia 3150
E-mail: info@blueangelonline.com
Website: www.blueangelonline.com

Edited by Jules Sutherland and Peter Loupelis

Blue Angel is a registered trademark of Blue Angel Gallery Pty. Ltd.

ISBN: 978-1-922573-84-1

Contents

WELCOME TO YOUR WILDNESS
Women Who Run from the Wolves 9
Dream Animals Unleash Our Power! 12
NOW is the Time! 13
Pray to Stop Being Prey 15
The Animals Have Had Enough 17
The Soul-ution 19
Why am I Writing This? 20
How to Work with Your *Wild Dreams Animal Oracle* 22
Card Layouts 28
Q & A 32

CARD MEANINGS
Bat 36
Bear 38
Bee 40
Big Cat 42
Bird 44
Buffalo 46
Bull 48
Butterfly 50
Cat 52
Chicken 54
Cow 56
Coyote 58
Crocodile 60
Deer 62
Dog 64

Dolphin 66
Dragonfly 68
Eagle 70
Elephant 72
Fish 74
Fox 76
Frog 78
Giraffe 80
Goat 82
Gorilla 84
Horse 86
Hummingbird 88
Insect 90
Monkey 92
Mouse 94
Octopus 96
Owl 98
Peacock 100
Pig 102
Rabbit 104
Shark 106
Skunk 108
Snake 110
Spider 112
Squirrel 114
Tortoise 116
Unicorn 118
Whale 120
Wolf 122

ABOUT THE AUTHOR 125
ABOUT THE ARTIST 127

WELCOME TO YOUR WILDNESS

How do you survive the wilderness?
Become the wilderness!

Women Who Run from the Wolves

It's graduation day, and excitement is in the air. A flare of joyous anticipation dances through the field of cap-and-gowned seniors, with family and friends cheering in the bleachers. I'm one of the graduates. I should be excited — so, what's with the lead in my belly?

Suddenly, the sky turns dark. I look way up at the man who has approached the elevated podium. It's President Snow, the evil nemesis from *The Hunger Games*, who happens to be the president of my school. He addresses the graduating seniors in a slow, evenly paced baritone that reverberates throughout the stadium, "I'd like to say how proud I am of our graduates and all their hard work. To demonstrate how much they've learned, BRING ON THE WOLVES!"

At his command, a thousand ravenous wolves burst onto the scene, snarling, growling, running toward us. In a flash, mayhem ensues. With a flurry of caps and gowns in the air, we all trample over each other, desperate to escape the horror.

The thought occurs to me: *I should demonstrate what I've learned by running toward the wolves.*

I then realize I'm flanked by Shadow and Lola, my pet dogs — who would be juicy snacks to the wolves. It becomes clear that I must flee the scene for their sake.

I throw the dogs in my truck and screech out of the

parking lot, knowing we are safe — for the moment. As I drive, it dawns on me: *I was never trained to deal with wolves! I'd better get trained!*

I awoke from this dream with a palpitating heart. I got up and lumbered to the bathroom, splashed water on my face, looked in the mirror, and told myself, "You were dreaming … but it's unfinished." I went back to bed with a plan — I needed to learn how to work with wolves.

Back asleep and back in the dream, I find myself standing in a field with the ravenous wolves — and I let them devour me. While being ripped to shreds, instead of feeling terrified, I surrender to an unexpected osmosis. I lose track of my ordinary, familiar self and hear the wolves communicate with one another. Next thing I know, I'm hunting with them, eating with them, loving them, howling at the moon with them … until eventually, *I am one of them.* Yet I'm still me — the wolf-woman version of me.

Suddenly, I'm back at the graduation ceremony, but now I'm the one standing at the podium. This time, the wolves that once chased me are lined up alongside and behind me. I don't speak with words — I command the space with my silence, standing in the strength of 1,000 wolves.

I awake feeling changed, charged, exponentially powerful, grounded, and ready to face any challenge life has in store for me.

. . .

The juxtaposition of this dream was magnificent. It came during a time of uncertainty in my career. My production team and I had pitched the round of networks on a dream TV show concept. We'd gotten close, but as they say, no cigar — and no green light. They said the show was "too soft". I'd also given away too much power caring what authority figures (network executives, symbolized by President Snow) had to say about me and my life.

Ha! If they'd only been in the dream I just had!

The rejection caused me to wonder: *Does the world really need another dream interpreter? Hasn't everything about dreams already been said? Am I too soft?*

Wolves, to me, are the ultimate symbol of wildness, being in touch with nature, and having the strength of a pack of like-minded soul beings. I interpreted this dream to mean I had graduated from putting the network executives (or any 'authority figure') on a pedestal. Instead, I became a more empowered version of myself. I was infused with an even deeper appreciation of the power of dreams.

Since that dream, I carry with me a sense of confidence and empowerment that no outward success or college degree could give me. I've experienced a soul shift, from feeling insecurity-ridden to becoming a force of nature in my own right — calling the shots in my own life.

Dream Animals Unleash Our Power!

All animals—big, small, underground, above ground, in the water, on the land, in the air, fine, feathered, or hairless—enter our dreams to inspire us to understand our particular animal totem and to claim our wildness. At the very least, animals romp into our nighttime dreams to help stop us from being so damn civilized and recognize the importance of making at least a little wiggle room in our fast-paced, high-tech, overly caffeinated lives to …

- Express our feelings.
- Move our bodies.
- Honor our instincts.
- Get out in nature.
- Eat when hungry.
- Pee when we feel the urge.
- Rest when tired.
- Run when inspired.
- Take time for pleasure.
- Make room for the parts of our personalities that might be deemed silly and socially unacceptable yet relate to our genius, vitality, and perhaps our greatest contribution to this world.

NOW is the Time!

This conversation—and this oracle deck—is timely and (dare I say) crucial because our humanity is at a crossroads. Technology has served us well in some ways. Many of us have more virtual friends than ever (via social networking), more virtual adventures (via video games), and more of a virtual platform for self-expression (via social media). But we've become more sedentary and out of balance than at any other time in history. In fact, our butts have never experienced such deeply ingrained chair marks.

In the Western world, so many of us are sick, depressed, medicated, addicted, in therapy, in debt, and unhappy — yet we've never had more of the stuff we claim we want. We've meandered so far outside our natural rhythm and our connection to the tides, the moon, and the land, that the animals are getting our attention the only way they can — in our dreams, where we are a captive audience. Via nighttime dreams, animals are swinging toward us on vines, running after us in packs, swimming with us in pods, flying around us in V-shaped lines — on a mission to call us back to balance … and they're not taking 'no' for an answer!

Now do you get why lions, tigers, bears, and whales are stalking you in your dreams?

You thought they were coming to harm or kill you — but they are not. They are coming to rescue you from living a life of quiet—or not-so-quiet—despair in their own signature way. Think of a mama lion whose cub is about to fall off a cliff. She doesn't ping her son via a text message to arrange a time for a civilized conversation over a nice, hot cup of tea. *No!* She pounces on him, pins him to the ground, smacks his head with her gigantic paws, and growls at him until he gets the message.

Pray to Stop Being Prey

> *Nearly all men can stand adversity, but if you want to test a man's character, give him power.*
> — ROBERT G. INGERSOLL

Running from animals in our dreams reflects that we are running from our power in our waking lives. We unconsciously think that if we could camouflage ourselves and blend into the background well enough, our power (animals) won't notice us. But our animals are on the scent — and like a dog with a bone, they are obsessed and won't stop until they catch us by the scruff of our necks and reunite us with our power!

We've become masterful at our elaborate avoidance skills. I believe that once upon a time, we had all our power intact, but we didn't know what to do with it. We didn't have the maturity or spiritual awareness to handle the responsibility, and thus we unknowingly misused it — hurting, injuring, and stepping on too many toes along the way. So, we decided it would be easier to 'play possum' in this lifetime, hide in a cave, fly away, bury our heads in the sand, or roll over and play dead rather than own our enormous power.

If we had to choose between victim or perpetrator, many of us—especially women—would choose victim. Not in every instance, of course, but many of us unconsciously think it's cute to be powerless because of the brownie points we've earned for it in the past. We scratch, claw, and fight like hell for our limitations, clinging to our mask as the inadequate, insecure, woe-is-me damsel in distress or sad sack guy that just can't catch a break. A part of us believes that by quivering in the corner of our flailing wimp-dom, other people will love us because they feel less inadequate around us. But this is not love! It's a snake pit disguised as an all-you-can-eat buffet — its poison will kill us if we don't get the antivenom, and quick.

The Animals Have Had Enough

The animals have a new motto: *No more playing nice.*

Your dreams may be the only time and place you're not a moving target — when you stop bobbing and weaving long enough for your animals to get a good shot at you. The good news about these 'chasing' dreams/nightmares—that indicate we've cut ourselves off from our power—is this: *If we can cut ourselves off, then we can reconnect ourselves.*

Imagine the moment of your birth. You were a perfect, whole, precious wild child. As you grew, you had to learn to become 'good' to fit in — nice, orderly, crossing your t's and dotting your i's. On top of that, with every trauma, moment of stress, or heartbreak you endured, a part of you—like a discarded puzzle piece—got lost in the bowels of your closet.

Some shamanic cultures (such as the Huichol people of Mexico) work with the concept of 'soul retrieval' — the process of reclaiming your lost puzzle pieces and putting them back together. I believe our 'chasing' dreams/nightmares are our missing puzzle pieces in animal form, seeking us out to reconnect and restore us to our original wholeness.

We think the menace/animal chasing us in our dreams is hell-bent on annihilating us, and perhaps to some degree, that is true. But I believe our dream animals only seek to eradicate our limited, flimsy, disempowered personas so that we can awaken to the beauty and bounty of our true selves. The only thing annihilated will be our egos and the ridiculous masks of victimhood hiding our radiant magnificence. Good riddance!

When we face and embrace the animals chasing us, we realize that which doesn't kill us makes us stronger — and that which does kill us transforms us.

. . .

As a dream expert, I have an inbox full of dreams people send me to decode. Yes, I read these while sitting on my chair-imprinted derriere. It's astounding to me the number of dreams that involve animals chasing people. Not a day goes by that I don't passionately reassure some worried person that instead of being shocked or scared, they should be grateful for their dream.

I tell them, "You're dreaming about this (lion, snake, bear, tiger, whale, bee), so you can reconnect with the power and genius you've desperately shoved into your personal 'Pandora's box'. The animals are chasing after you to help you realign with your nature, so you can come back to balance with your body, mind, and soul."

The Soul-ution

What if the *soul-ution* is so simple it's breathing down your neck, flying just overhead, or panting at your feet? What if being in touch with your inner animal—your wild soulfulness—is the solution to thriving, not just surviving?

    I'm not saying toss all technology out. Of course not. This card deck would not exist without the latest, greatest, most sophisticated, cutting-edge technology. What I am saying is that making time—at least five minutes a day—to tune in and shine the light of your awareness on your inner animal could make all the difference to your health, vitality, magnetism, charisma, manifesting, and relationships — not to mention your sex life.

Why am I Writing This?

> *Most people rarely align with their true power, because it seems illogical to them that there is power in relaxation, in letting go, or in love or joy or bliss.*
> — ABRAHAM (as channeled by Esther Hicks)

I once met a woman who lived on a horse ranch in Malibu, California. The moment we met, she told me, "I don't trust humans. I only trust animals. They don't have egos, so they don't lie."

"Nice to meet you too," I thought sarcastically.

Even though I was shocked by what she said, I realized how much truth there was in her brash words. Animals don't lie. And then I realized: *neither do dreams*. We can trust them both to set off alarm bells when we've become too engrossed in our civilized pomp and circumstance. The animals in our dreams are the ultimate gift, wake-up call, and invitation for us to become stewards of our power.

After encountering this woman, I began tracking my animal dreams and noticed the animals were emerging in droves. Over the next few years, I had more wolf dreams—like the one I shared in the introduction—and before that, dreams featuring dolphins, bees, and dragonflies, not to mention my dogs Woofie, Shadow, Lola, and Priya — who are all my spirit allies from the other side now.

The dragonfly dreams led me to marry my husband and connected me with other souls who became significant in my life, especially those with dragonfly tattoos. The dolphin dreams helped me improve my eyesight, and the bee dreams helped me stop being so busy and learn to be queenlier in my life. Dreams of my pet dogs helped me open my heart and find more unconditional love for myself and others. The wolf dreams showed up when I needed to channel my anger and graduate to a more empowered state.

Because of these dreams, I realized that what is suppressed must be expressed. Yet I fiercely desired to live by the credo 'do no harm'. I imagine you have this yearning, too.

So, how do we express ourselves fully, not hurt anyone, keep relationships thriving, maintain stability, and behave in a way others would deem lovable so we can be accepted yet still be wild?

That is a tall order.

And I believe our animal dreams are helping us find our way through the complexity of being both freedom and harmony-seeking beings, civilized and uncivilized, tame and untamable.

WHAT WOULD THE ANIMALS SAY?
We're here to remind you that you're alive, sexual, sensual, and instinctual, with a pulse. You deserve to be fed, move your body, and have nature in your life … because your nature is an integral part of life. Because when you are out of balance, the entire jungle, forest, wetlands, sky, and oceans suffer. But once you embrace your inner animal, nature is restored, and you are more inclined to honor the entire natural world. When you return home to yourself, like the prodigal child, a feast will await you, and we can thrive and celebrate once again.

How to Work with Your "Wild Dreams Animal Oracle"

This deck features animal wisdom to:

- **Springboard** your intuition.
- **Illuminate** your ability to interpret your nighttime dreams.
- **Amplify** your higher guidance.
- **Wake up** your wisdom.
- **Activate** your boldness and empower your waking life.

The cards are alphabetized in this guidebook, and you will find a keynote, inspirational quote, message, meaning, manifestation, and mantra for each. This text will help you deepen your relationship with the animals you encounter in your waking life as well as in your dreams.

Animal's Message — *What the chosen animal would say if it could speak English.*
When you draw this card in a reading, this is the animal's advice to you.

Meaning — *Interpretation of the animal in your waking or sleeping dream.*
From the perspective that we dream all the time, this section addresses the animal when it crosses your path in your daytime reality. Also, when you have a sleep-time dream about an animal, consider this interpretation

of what it may mean for you. The rule of thumb with dream interpretation is that you are the ultimate authority on what your dreams are telling you. Allow these suggested interpretations to entice your wisdom to the surface.

Manifestation — *Action to embody the animal's wisdom.*
Every remembered dream requires action in your waking world. This section is a guide to a suggested action you can take to honor the animals in your dream and integrate their essence into your life.

Mantra — *A thought to carry with you as a touchstone throughout your day.*
A short, affirmative statement to anchor the essence of the animal and the card in your daily life. Repeat the mantra silently in contemplative meditation or memorize it so you can repeat it to yourself. Allow the mantra to color your thoughts and align you with your most awakened self.

BLESS YOUR CARDS

To make the most of your experience with your *Wild Dreams Animal Oracle*, begin by blessing your cards. You can do this once upon opening your deck and/or before you initiate a reading. There are many ways to bless your cards. Here are some suggestions:

- Light a candle.
- Burn sage or incense.
- Sprinkle the cards with salt.
- Speak a blessing/prayer out loud or silently to yourself. Choose a blessing you are comfortable with. I have included one here that you may like to try:

God/Goddess, beloved dream maker, Holy Spirit, heavenly guides, and animal spirits: Thank you for always supporting me in the highest way. With each exhale, I clean the slate of my mind and these cards. With each new breath, I open the portals of my heart, mind, body, and soul to align with the wisdom of my animal helpers. May the cards I'm drawn to in this reading catalyze my inner knowing and point to the best way to perceive and engage with my life. May the cards I draw support me, and/or whoever I am reading for, in awakening sacred wildness. Direct me to steward my power wisely, compassionately, and always for the highest good of all. A-men. A-women. A-humans. A-animals. A-dreams!

REVERSE CARDS

If you pull an upside-down card, consider that it may be bringing up an issue in your blind spot — perhaps a shadow or an unintegrated aspect of yourself. Rejoice in this blessed opportunity to bring your power (genius, talent, energy) that has been concealed into the light of your awareness.

CONSCIOUSLY WORKING WITH YOUR CARDS

The moments bookending your sleep are when the veil between worlds is thinnest. I think of these moments as prime real estate. You can draw cards from your *Wild Dreams Animal Oracle* anytime, but the wisdom of your dreaming mind is most accessible right before bed and as you are waking. Here are some tips for how to connect with this potent guidance:

Before Sleep

As you tuck yourself into bed, become centered by taking several deep breaths, then:

- Contemplate an issue in your life in need of divine guidance. You might want to journal about this or simply meditate on the specific intent of your dream declaration. (For more on this, see my book *It's All in Your Dreams: 5 Portals to an Awakened Life*).
- Invite guidance from who/whatever you consider a source of divine power (e.g., God/Goddess, angels, spirit guides, the Universe, etc.) to help you choose the card that best supports you to gain insight into the issue.

- Meditate on the card's message, dream symbol, and mantra for a few moments. Allow this meditation to lead you into a wonderful dream time.

Upon Waking

Here's a suggested ritual for starting your day:

- On waking, record your dreams in a journal, writing pad, or app on your phone.
- Record at least a line or two about what you think your dream means and its message for you.
- Contemplate the intention you set before bed (your dream declaration) and see if you can perceive how your dream's wisdom applies.
- Shuffle the *Wild Dreams Animal Oracle* cards and spread them out, face down, in front of you. While contemplating your dream declaration and/or any question about your dream (e.g., "What were the wolves trying to tell me?"), select a card. Look it up alphabetically in this guidebook. Read through its insights and meditate on its mantra and image for a few minutes.
- As you move through your day, note any synchronicities related to the animal on your card, your dream, your dream declaration, or all of the above.

For Therapists, Coaches, or Dream Workers

To assist your clients in accessing a deeper insight or spiritual awareness of the signs and symbols around them:

- Ask your client to identify a question or issue on which they would like guidance.
- Offer them the oracle deck by spreading it out, face down, and have them choose a card.
- Let them read the card's message, meaning, manifestation, and mantra.
- Encourage them to identify any insights, thoughts, or feelings evoked by the animal, its image, or its message as it relates to where they are in their lives. Hold space for your client to make their own associations and draw their own conclusions.
- Once your client has expressed their initial hunch about what they feel the card(s) are saying to them, offer your insights.
- Then support your client to do the manifestation process there with you. Once it's completed, ask them to share any further insights and share your own accordingly.
- Finish the session by suggesting any other action steps your client can take to anchor the wisdom of their *Wild Dreams Animal Oracle* card.

Card Layouts

DAILY ORACLE

The most basic, on-the-go way to access your *Wild Dreams Animal Oracle* is with a single-card reading. Here is a step-by-step method to help you get the most from your one-card layout.

1. **Close your eyes and take several deep breaths.**

2. **Shuffle the cards as you contemplate a question, such as:**
   - What's important for me to pay attention to right now?
   - What is in my blind spot?
   - What should I focus on today?
   - What is my message for the day?
   - What should I do about _____?
   - What is the gift/blessing/lesson in the situation I'm in right now?
   - What do I need to become aware of in my creative endeavors/relationships/health/finances/spirituality?
   - What aspect of my recent dream is most important for me to pay attention to?

3. **Select the card that feels right to you.**
   With the cards facing away from you, select the card you feel most drawn to. If you'd like, close your eyes, and move your hands an inch above the cards. You might

feel a rise or fall in temperature, or a tingling sensation as your hand hovers over a particular card. Your hand might 'accidentally' brush against a card. Sometimes, a card might even fall off the table or flip over. There doesn't need to be fireworks — you can select a card randomly. However it happens, the card you choose is the card for you.

4. **Meditate upon the card's image, keynote, inspirational quote, message, meaning, and mantra.**

5. **Take a few minutes to do the suggested action steps in the manifestation to bring the animal's wisdom to life.**

6. **Carry the card with you throughout the day.**
   Place the card in your pocket or purse, on your desk or refrigerator, or by your bathroom mirror (for the day) to remind you of the wisdom of your animal.

THREE-CARD LAYOUT

This spread is helpful for gaining clarity on the larger story of your life or an issue you face, and to trigger possible solutions. The cards can be read as past, present, and future; or as issue, resolution, and outcome.

Pick three cards and lay them in front of you, left to right:

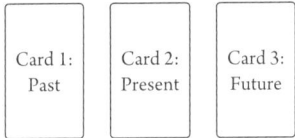

Card 1: Your past or a challenge you've been facing.
Card 2: Your present or possible response to the current issue.
Card 3: Your future or the likely result.

FOUR-CARD LAYOUT

Use this spread for problem-solving and conflict resolution.

Pick four cards and lay them in front of you, left to right:

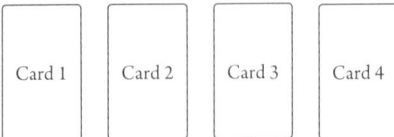

Card 1: Insight about the conflict.
Card 2: Insight into your part of the equation for which you are responsible.
Card 3: Insight into the other person's part of the equation for which they are responsible.

Card 4: Insight into the gift, lesson, and/or blessing in disguise in this interaction for both parties.

Q & A

Q: Are there any good or bad cards?
A: All the cards are good, important, and valuable, which is true for every dream and every animal. That doesn't mean your ego won't judge certain cards as more fortuitous than others. The truth is, each card comes with its challenges and blessings. The determining factor in whether you get a 'good' or 'bad' reading is your ability to honor your intuition and the wisdom gleaned from the card. Remember, what you do with the cards you draw (i.e., how you interpret them) makes all the difference.

Q: How can I work with the images?
A: The images, gorgeously created by Lisa Desimini, speak volumes. When you meditate upon the image of your card, pay attention to any part of it that stands out to you and how it makes you feel.

. . .

May this oracle deck lead you on a deeper dive into the heart of what the animal kingdom and queendom are trying to communicate to you.

May it also deepen your ability to deliberately dream with these free creatures and let them enhance your dreaming consciousness — for greater freedom of your wild spirit and undomesticated self-expression.

May your wildest and most wonderful dreams come true. And may the full potency of the animal kingdom and queendom within you reach its most conscious, empowered, and joyous expression. As you are lifted, may all be lifted!

Kelly

. . .

CARD MEANINGS

Bat

**The more you love the mystery,
the more it reveals its secrets.**

*The world is wrong side up. It needs to be turned upside down
in order to be right side up.*
— BILLY SUNDAY

BAT'S MESSAGE
If you're feeling lost, upside down, and like everything has gone dark, open your inner eyes and behold your life circumstances from Bat's point of view. When life flips upside down, consider that it may be right side up. Though unsettling for your ego, being in unknown territory can be tonic for the soul and an opportunity for hidden dimensions of your spirit to be revealed.

MEANING
Bat medicine represents rebirth, reincarnation, transition, intuition, and your ability to find your way through any dark night into the light. Don't worry if your blind ambition has caused you to bump into walls. Once you're on the other side of the obstacle you're currently working through, you will not only be unflappable but also discover a treasure-laden gateway to a new dimension of purpose in your life.

MANIFESTATION
On a sheet of paper, draw or sketch an issue that you've been struggling with. Don't worry if you're not Picasso. Draw with stick figures if you have to. When you're done, flip it upside down and notice what you see. The process of turning your story on its head has the potential to open the floodgates of your *i-magic-nation* to perceive the insights that have been here all along. This simple shift in perspective can activate your latent wisdom to help you navigate your batty situation toward grace and blessings galore.

MANTRA
My inner sonar attunes me to high-vibe guidance.

Bear

**You have the strength and resources
to bear whatever comes your way.**

The cave you fear to enter holds the treasures you seek.
— JOSEPH CAMPBELL

BEAR'S MESSAGE

When life feels too much to bear, give yourself a time-out and know Bear is here for you. Call on Bear when you need to face the unbearable … even if it is to behold how beautiful you are. Indulge in your well-earned cave-time by taking the opportunity to lay low, heal, and eat healthy food. Take heart in knowing you are storing up your reserves so when the time comes to act, you'll be ready. After you've had plenty of beauty sleep—which is highly productive, by the way—and are no longer running on fumes, you'll emerge with more energy and *for-bear-ance* to engage in life beyond your cave.

MEANING
Bears in dreams are a powerful symbol of strength, protection, and power. Bear's appearance can remind you that you have more reserves than you realize to withstand the challenges you are currently moving through. Your inner bear knows when to forage to ensure your basic needs get met, and it knows when to hibernate in a cuddly wintertime slumber. It also knows when to stand on its hind legs and roar when boundaries have been crossed too often.

MANIFESTATION
Take time for self-care—without having to get sick to do so—free from worry or *em-bear-assment*. Give yourself the bear hug you've been wanting from others, then hibernate and tend to the bare essentials of your life. Consider this card your permission slip to set boundaries so you can rest guilt-free. Once you get the rest you need, you'll feel inspired to shed your heavy coat of worries and emerge to play and dance in the sunlight of your life again.

MANTRA
I can bear anything as long as I get the cave-time I require.

Bee

Buzz with the sweetness of your most golden life.

Words are like bees — some create honey, and others leave a sting.
— UNKNOWN

BEE'S MESSAGE

There are queen bees, wanna-bees, and those with the spiritual fortitude to just simply be. Which will you be today? As many in the Western world do, you may have fallen for the buzz of over-valuing 'doing' more than 'being'. But you may not realize that actual productivity stems from being present in life, not just being busy for busy's sake. Bee's message for you is to be an 'enlightened opportunist'. In other words, don't waste time remaining stuck in the thorns and brambles of life — instead, beeline straight for the nectar in every circumstance.

MEANING

You've chosen this card to remind you that you are an alchemist who can turn a sticky situation into honey that sustains you, your hive, and life beyond your colony. Just as bees are essential in assisting flowers and plants to grow by cross-pollination, you can curate the grains of pollen (wisdom) you receive from your various life experiences and blend them into your unique ambrosia. If you are stung by a bee in dreams, it may reflect that someone's criticism or biting comment has left its mark on you. Your own inner critic may have also inflicted this. If this resonates, take heart in knowing you can pull the stinger out and heal. Once the pain subsides, fly toward the Eden of self-love and let the honey of your life overflow.

MANIFESTATION

Close your eyes, take a breath, and enter the 'Palace of Pollen' — your sanctuary within. Put your hand on your heart and feel the pulse of your soul essence reverberating through your body. Contemplate who and what you desire to 'be' in this life. Swarm with the strength of hive-mind — the exponential power of working side by side with resonant beings, whether physical or non-physical. Know that the sweetness of your beingness serves a higher purpose than you realize.

MANTRA

I share my inner nectar with myself and those my sweetness will fortify.

Big Cat

It's time to rule.

The greatest fear in the world is of the opinions of others. And the moment you are unafraid of the crowd you are no longer a sheep, you become a lion. A great roar arises in your heart, the roar of freedom.
— OSHO

BIG CAT'S MESSAGE

It's time for you to take your place as king or queen of the jungle. Your days of napping in the weeds are over. Big Cat's message is for you to unleash your power and claim your territory. Feel the strength of your (spiritual) muscles flexing, the vibration of your inner growl resounding in your chest, and your senses sharpening. Remember, leadership isn't about you — it's about the people you lead and the principles for which you stand.

The best leaders are the ones who follow a higher calling and subsequently inspire and empower others to do and become more than they thought they could. When you step into your purpose, others will follow in your pawprints — not for your sake, but for their own.

MEANING

If you dream about Big Cat (lion, tiger, ocelot, panther, cougar, jaguar, etc.), then know it is time for your inner hero to claim its space. Big Cat symbolizes your ferocious authority and ability to manifest what you need on behalf of your tribe. Instead of being terrified, when Big Cat pounces into your dreamscape, know they've come to infuse you with a boost of confidence and courage to do what only you can. Don't hold back — trust that the time has come to own your incredible power and wield it for the greater good.

MANIFESTATION

Create a mission statement articulating the guiding principles upon which you stand. For example: "My mission is to be a beneficial presence on the earth — to live a life of such inspiration, love, and contribution that everyone I meet is uplifted." Meditate on this every day and consult it in times of uncertainty. By doing this, when the time comes, and the spotlight appears, you'll be prepared to roar a hearty 'yes' as you seize the opportunity to share the beauty in your heart. Don't be surprised when passionate supporters begin to rally.

MANTRA

I embody my purpose, and my roar resounds throughout the jungle of life!

Bird

Like an angel, you fly when you take yourself lightly.

Birds were created to record everything. They were not designed just to be beautiful jewels in the sky but to serve as the eyes of heaven.
— SUZY KASSEM

BIRD'S MESSAGE

There's a time to be pragmatic and grounded, and this ain't it. Now is the time to use your mighty wingspan to break free from any constraints that have kept you stuck or weighed down. Allow Bird medicine to show you how to transcend the actual or perceived glass ceiling. Visualize yourself flying to new heights as you fulfill your creative, professional, and spiritual potential.

MEANING
Dreams of Bird are a message of freedom to help you explore the height, breadth, and wonder of your spiritual reality within the dream of your human incarnation. Birds often appear in dreams as a reward, symbolizing that you have risen above your challenges. Think of these dreams as a celebration of your state of mastery and grace, like an all-expenses-paid vacation that you've earned. Enjoy these dreams as they help elevate your consciousness to new, beckoning vistas.

MANIFESTATION
Einstein is believed to have observed that a problem can't be solved with the same level of thinking that created it. In other words, meditate on how good it would feel to rise above your obstacles and see the world from a more elevated perch. Notice how tiny your obstacles become when viewed from a sky-high perspective. Allow your bird's-eye consciousness to illuminate the possibilities beyond the horizon. Revel in feelings of peace, ease, and ecstatic expansiveness.

MANTRA
I fly beyond the nest of my comfort zone into the wild blue yonder of my greatest dreams.

Buffalo

Prosperity thunders through you.

*Cows run away from the storm while the buffalo charges toward it—
and gets through it quicker. Whenever I'm confronted with a tough
challenge, I do not prolong the torment, I become the buffalo.*
— WILMA MANKILLER

BUFFALO'S MESSAGE
You have more going for you than you may think. When you
align with Great Spirit, the earth, sky, wind, and rain orchestrate
life in your favor. Be mindful of your power. When you give
your whole self to the task at hand, you will prevail with great
abundance.

MEANING
Because buffalo are so powerful with such a giant head, they are considered mindful, thoughtful, and intelligent. However, buffalo can be hot-headed, unpredictable, and dangerous when provoked. You've chosen this card as a message to release your frustration in a positive, life-serving way. Keep in mind, many Native American nations of the Great Plains—such as the Lakota—believe the buffalo is so sacred that when hunted, every part of the animal is used to its full potential. The message here is to take stock of your gifts, talents, and resources and not let them go to waste.

MANIFESTATION
Contemplate your goal. See it as if it were a giant red target at the center of the universe. Call to mind all the resources—people, circumstances, and experiences—you have available to help you fulfill your dream. Raise your horns toward the sky and align with your highest wisdom. Funnel the energy stored in your physical and psychic bodies toward your desire.

MANTRA
I have everything it takes to hit my mark with grace and ease.

Bull

Hold your ground.

I shall not be moved.
— AFRICAN-AMERICAN SPIRITUAL AND PROTEST SONG
(famously recorded by Mississippi John Hurt)

BULL'S MESSAGE

Embrace your masculine (yang) energy to stand firm on issues you're passionate about. If you're already the dominant type, think (and maybe even take a ballet lesson) before you act, and channel your strength—and bullishness—toward a cause greater than yourself. However, if you are a shrinking violet, consider this your permission slip to assert yourself. The time for waiting is over. Take the bull by the horns, conjure your strength, and charge ahead — and if a few plates in the china shop break, so be it. After all, breakdowns lead to breakthroughs.

MEANING

Let Bull medicine help you focus your personal power to finish a task or stand by your convictions. Dreams of Bull are a message that you are finding your inner strength. Stand still and let your potency, bravery, and steadfastness manifest on the earth plane toward a healthy, wealthy life.

MANIFESTATION

Call to mind an area of life in which you would like to take a greater stand. Think of three steps that you can take to be more proactive about putting your passion in action. Now do one of them today.

MANTRA

I release attachment to the bull#&%* and act on what matters most.

Butterfly

It's time for radical transformation.

I dreamed I was a butterfly, flitting around in the sky; then I awoke. Now I wonder: Am I a man who dreamt of being a butterfly, or am I a butterfly dreaming that I am a man?
— CHUANG TZU

BUTTERFLY'S MESSAGE

You are of the earth, yet you are so much more. You were born to fly. As challenging as your current meltdown may be, it's underrated. While you struggle toward sovereignty, you are building the muscle you'll need to navigate the freedom and awe-inspiring beauty of your unprecedented future. Let yourself be reborn today, knowing you are constantly evolving to become your genuine, spiritually liberated self. Trust the process. You are more expansive than you ever dreamed possible.

MEANING
Because butterflies move through such archetypal transformation—from the caterpillar through the chrysalis to a winged creature—they symbolize unforeseeable change, freedom, expansion, and full self-expression. When Butterfly appears in your dream, it's a message to embrace all the cycles of your life, especially whatever is happening in the present moment. This card may come as a reminder that you are awakening from the perceived confines of your mortal shackles to discover your spiritual inheritance — the full scope of your heavenly gifts.

MANIFESTATION
Take a few minutes to meditate upon the butterfly version of yourself. Stand with arms and legs spread wide, your head lifted toward the sky. Feel a lightness of being, and the (real or imagined) wind beneath you, carrying you to wherever you desire. As you emerge from this meditation, keep Butterfly's energy with you. Go ahead and show off. As they say, "If you've got it, flaunt it!" Wear your brightest colors today because this is a precious moment, a time you've worked hard for. Fully enjoy — this is the season of your just desserts.

MANTRA
The splendor of my multi-colored wings flies me to the realm of my fully orbed dream life.

Cat

Stop trying so hard — you're already purrrrfect.

*Way down deep, we're all motivated by the same urges.
Cats just have the courage to live by them.*
— JIM DAVIS

CAT'S MESSAGE
Be more self-sourced and sovereign when it comes to your needs. Follow your pleasure principle and trust where it leads. Consider the possibility that what is innately good for you might be (ultimately) *cat-egorically* good for all. In other words, when you are your most authentic—as opposed to your most domesticated—your inner motor purrs in contentment and becomes contagious. It's okay to take a leap into uncharted

territory and know that even if it doesn't work out the way you hope, it will be a *cat-apult* toward a new incarnation of your creative spirit.

MEANING
Dreams of Cat are symbolic of your feminine sensuality. Cats are known as shapeshifters and travelers between the third, fourth, and fifth dimensions. They also travel seamlessly between needing others as a scratching post—or a place for affection and attention—and guilt-free solo wanderlust time. Consider Cat's appearance in your dream as a *cat-a-lyst* for greater attunement to your intuition and psychic abilities. Because you innately know you are invincible—with at least nine lives—you can take more risks.

MANIFESTATION
Rest more, worry less ... so when you're ready to pounce, you'll do so with precision. At the very least, indulge in a catnap today, so when it's time to leap, you'll have the wherewithal to land on your feet.

MANTRA
It's time for me-e-oww time — and when inspired, I'll leap boldly into the mystery.

Chicken

**You are the alpha and the omega,
the chicken and the egg.**

*I dream of a better tomorrow, where chickens can cross the road
and not be questioned about their motives.*
— RALPH WALDO EMERSON

CHICKEN'S MESSAGE
Feeling cooped up? Choosing this card may be a message to rise early in the morning — or do what you must to make time for yourself beyond your flock. Regardless of the time, imagine it's the dawn of a new day, and you have a blank slate before you. All restrictions from the past are just feathers in the wind. So, stop putting all your eggs in one basket. It's time to shake your tail,

diversify your self-expression and let your unique personality shine. If you need more time to nest and rest until you feel ready to hatch your big plan, give that to yourself — and when you're ready, ruffle your feathers and express your wild self.

MEANING
Chicken is an emblem of fertility, so when one struts into your dream, it may be a message to join the flock and be more social. If you've been overly chicken (holding yourself back), flighty (avoiding facing the unavoidable challenges on your path), or feeling henpecked (allowing someone's critical remarks to fence you in), this might be a message to come home to roost. Get yourself a wing person because you are stronger when two or more flock together.

MANIFESTATION
Chickens are vocal creatures with their warbles and clucks. Write or voice record stream-of-consciousness, and let all your inner gibberish (fear) be released. Once you clear the blah-blah-blah of your mind chatter, identify one or two things you are grateful for, along with the eggs (ideas/projects/ventures) you are hatching. Release your fear so your communication can be made from a clear and grounded place. Keep in mind that you're just beginning to scratch the surface of your great contribution.

MANTRA
I allow my community and life itself to be the wind at my back and beneath my wings.

Cow

Moove when moved.

A babe is fed with milk and praise.
— CHARLES LAMB

COW'S MESSAGE

You are *udderly* fantastic. It's time for you not to be just the nurturer but the nurtured. Your needs are as important as everyone else's. Take a break and nourish your mind, body, and spirit. This card is a message for you to receive the kindness of the world and milk it for all it's worth, so you'll in turn have more to give.

MEANING
Cow, as the ultimate symbol of sacredness, providence, fertility, and motherhood, invites you to love more fully. When Cow grazes across your dream it may be a message to receive the TLC you've been so freely giving others so that you can enjoy more prosperity in your projects, babies, and/or relationships. This gentle spirit is the emblem of protection in many cultures and gives you the message to take heart. The storm you are in will pass, and you will be okay. Stand in your power, as you remember — the softest energies are not weak. Like tides and moonlight, their cycles rule the world.

MANIFESTATION
Sometimes we give what we most desire to receive. Make a list of the gifts you are known in your herd for providing, i.e., support, presence, reliability, creativity, humor, joy, or empathy. Ask yourself, which of those qualities do you need most right now? Instead of waiting for someone else to give that to you, get creative about how you will fill yourself with some of the nurturing you've been so generously giving to others.

MANTRA
Holy cow! The pasture is truly greenest right where I am.

Coyote

Expect the unexpected.

*Learn the rules like a pro,
so you can break them like an artist.*
— PABLO PICASSO

COYOTE'S MESSAGE

Just when you expect life to unfold in a predictable, sensible, organized manner, it flips upside down — and that's okay. You will find life-changing shamanic wisdom in the most unexpected places and circumstances. Your innate adaptability will help you be flexible and adjust gracefully to situations you did not see coming. Even when you find yourself in what seems like a Mercury Retrogradian detour, remember — Spirit has a plan for you that's a million times better than the one you had for yourself.

MEANING
Because Coyote is stealthy, it only reveals itself when you are being initiated into your next level of spiritual growth. Dreams of Coyote connect you to unconventional ways you get your needs met, so you can take any power back that you've given away. Consider how Coyote medicine is teaching you to be nimble, adaptable, and playful. When Coyote shows up on your path, let them inspire you to greet life's surprises with open arms and a baked cake.

MANIFESTATION
When was the last time you laughed until you cried? Be on the hunt for the hilarious and on the prowl for your inner prankster. If nothing immediately appears, then go hunting for it. Take five minutes and create a 'Funny Folder' — a file filled with silly memes or videos that tickle your inner coyote's funny bone. Open your Funny Folder when you've gotten trapped into taking life too seriously. If you can keep your sense of humor—even when snared in life's most challenging moments—you will prevail.

MANTRA
Even when events unfold differently than I planned, I trust in the divine order of life.

Crocodile

Take a bite out of your fear.

There is strong shadow where there is much light.
— JOHANN WOLFGANG VON GOETHE

CROCODILE'S MESSAGE

Own all your power, even that which does not look pretty. If you've been burying deep-seated feelings, instincts, or resentments, realize that they can't fester there forever without taking a toll on you. If there is no outlet for your feelings, they will eventually bubble up to the surface and *SNAP!* Heads will roll. Your intense feelings are valid and come from a pure, instinctual place — they are usually about protecting you and your loved ones when survival is at stake. However, if you've been finding yourself in the swamp of negativity, recycling and stewing on issues, or being quick to temper, this may be a message to take responsibility for your impact on those around you.

MEANING

The last thing most people think of when they call to mind a crocodile is its maternal energy. You might be surprised to know that they are fierce protectors of their babies. Yes, Crocodile can be cold-blooded, but that is to ensure survival, not only of itself but of those in its care. Crocodile's message in waking and sleeping dreams is to pay attention to the protective power lurking just beneath the surface of your sweet, kind, charming personality. Your crocodile aspect may have been relegated to the shadows because of its knack for surprise attacks. But Crocodile is a powerful ally when you need to plot the best course of action for yourself and your loved ones.

MANIFESTATION

Give yourself an outlet by venting the full-throttle intensity of your emotions in your journal. Ask yourself, "Who am I trying to protect?" and "What is the good intent beneath my anger?" Once you've drained the swamp of toxic feelings, when it's time to open your mouth and express yourself, say what you mean — without having to say it mean.

MANTRA

I discover beauty in the most unlikely places.

Deer

Honor your sensitivity as your greatest strength.

My feet will tread soft as a deer in the forest …
My heart will be strong as a great oak.
— JULIET MARILLIER

DEER'S MESSAGE

Dear one, if you've been feeling caught in the headlights, be kind but firm with yourself while you move out of the road into your inner sanctuary. Once you are in the loving arms of your safe haven, reconnect with your delicate, graceful nature and remember that your sensitivity is a virtue. Reclaim your harmonious balance with the natural world, and your gift for keen perception will guide you toward higher frequencies of light.

MEANING
Encounters with deer fill us with awe because we intuitively know we're receiving an infusion of healing, grace, innocence, and permission to follow our intuition. Allow Deer's bright spirit to nuzzle and give you a respite from the harshness of life while reclaiming the joy, strength, and freedom of your authentic being. When this gentle spirit reveals itself in your dreams, you are awakening to your wise and tender heart.

MANIFESTATION
Take a day to be dear to yourself. If you can't take an entire day, at least carve out a couple of hours (or minutes) to luxuriate in the quietest place you can find, ideally in nature. If that's not available to you, then dip into an Epsom salt bath and allow the hot water to relax you and give your fight/flight responses a break. As your nervous system adjusts to the nourishing effect of the water, you'll be able to return to grazing in the meadow of your greatest possibilities.

MANTRA
I navigate my world with sure-footed grace and honor for all life.

Dog

**Be loyal to those
who are loyal to you.**

*If you want someone who will listen to you every time,
do everything you tell them to do, and always be there for you
for better or for worse, get a dog.*
— ANONYMOUS

DOG'S MESSAGE

Just because you know the rules doesn't mean you can't bend (or break) them when your instincts tell you to. Your loyalty is a sacred gift that enhances the lives of everyone to whom you devote yourself — but the person who deserves your fidelity most is you. This card may be a nip at your heels to be more attuned to your intuition so you can joyously sniff out the best ways to meet your needs.

MEANING
Dogs in dreams represent the part of you that is in this world but not of it. Your dog aspect is innately wild—a direct descendant of the wolf—and yet it knows its way around the human realm. Dogs show up in dreams to give you an injection of best friend support. This dog encounter may be due to your inner tug-of-war between freedom and harmony, the duality of the desire to be a part of a pack, and the yearning to be your own top dog. This dream may also be barking at you to set boundaries with someone in your life.

MANIFESTATION
Take a few minutes today to play like it's your job. Get on the floor (if applicable) or go outside, roll in the grass, jump through the sprinklers, or lap up every last drop of your favorite meal. At the very least, indulge your senses by taking a huge whiff of something that pleases you — perfume, essential oils, or chocolate chip cookies. Notice how your sense of smell and taste invigorates your entire sensory being.

MANTRA
I pat myself on the back for being true blue to my most instinctual self.

Dolphin

Flow in the ecstatic tides of life.

*Follow your bliss, and the universe
will open doors where there were only walls.*
— JOSEPH CAMPBELL

DOLPHIN'S MESSAGE
You are invited to celebrate your life. Regardless of any temporary setbacks you may be navigating, you can always find a reason to leap out of the water in a passionate aerial flip of pure, unbridled joy. Stop downplaying your excitement about the many things going swimmingly well for you in your life. The more you dance, splash, and twirl throughout your day, the more reasons you will discover to celebrate!

MEANING
When you dream of Dolphin, allow yourself to feel as if you've witnessed a miracle. Dolphins are considered by many to be a more advanced species than our own, and they offer us a path to enlightenment by encouraging our attunement with their heart-expanding bliss. Because dolphins can see clearly underwater—and water, in the language of dreams, is emotion—this dream may be a message to see through any tumultuous feelings to the treasure (wisdom/guidance/insight) beneath the surface.

MANIFESTATION
Look for a reason to celebrate today. Even if it seems silly or unwarranted, literally write on your calendar, "Today is a day to celebrate my life!" Now look for the reasons to celebrate and invite your pod-mates to celebrate with you.

MANTRA
I blissipline *myself to see the miraculous and celebration-worthy in every moment.*

Dragonfly

Bring your reality to your dreams.

The dragonfly brings dreams to reality and is the messenger of wisdom and enlightenment from other realms.
— UNKNOWN

DRAGONFLY'S MESSAGE

You are a magical being — so much so that you chose this card to remind yourself it's time to fly. We dragonflies live in the third, fourth, and fifth dimensions and help humans elevate their consciousness to the state where magic and miracles are commonplace. In other words, no matter what is going on—as heavy as it may seem—when you drop your baggage, ego, personal agenda, and attachments to an outcome, you can dance with the wind and ascend to higher ground. Don't be fooled by appearances — although you may feel small, you are anything but.

MEANING

When Dragonfly enters your dream, it is a blessing, reminding you that you are as mighty as a dragon in disguise, fueled by the power of both this world and the world beyond the veil. You are here to reveal a transformed way of seeing and being. Your inner dragonfly can see through any challenge to the beauty that lies beneath. A miniature version of Dragon, Dragonfly also embodies the symbol of power, strength, and good luck for those worthy of its support. You pulled this card as proof that you are worthy.

MANIFESTATION

When you find yourself feeling small, look in the mirror, take a deep breath, gaze at your reflection, and see the entire universe beaming back at you through your eyes. Allow this awareness to give you the boost in confidence you need to transform your earthly experience into a heavenly one.

MANTRA

I celebrate my joyous, light-hearted nature, knowing all the magic of the universe is within me!

Eagle

Fly on the wings of your higher purpose.

As an eagle, weary after soaring in the sky, folds its wings and flies down to rest in its nest, so does the shining Self enter the state of dreamless sleep, where one is freed from all desires.
— BRIHADARANYAKA UPANISHAD

EAGLE'S MESSAGE

Eagle's perspective is 180 degrees different from your ego's. To help you align with your most high-flying self, allow Eagle to carry you up where you belong. Hang on tight as you fly to the heavens and back. Attune your intentions with the higher plane, and you will manifest (and *dream-a-fest*) a most heavenly life — for you and all those in your convocation. Once you've acclimated to a higher vibration and it's time to come down to earth, you will do so with clarity, precision, efficiency, and intent.

MEANING

Because eagles soar high in the sky, they are considered by many to be the king of the birds. Associated with qualities of bravery and honor, they come into your dream to bestow upon you the gift of vision and intuition. In fact, according to legend, when the brazen crow pecks on the eagle's back, the eagle doesn't become stressed, agitated, or get its feathers ruffled. Instead, it sets its gaze higher and flies to a loftier altitude (attitude). Soon, the crow falls off the eagle's back due to a lack of oxygen. Thus, when life stresses you out, don't fight fire with fire — instead, rise to a higher level of consciousness, and you'll realize there are no battles to fight.

MANIFESTATION

Call to mind an issue that's been challenging you. Imagine that issue is a crow/raven on your back. Imagine yourself as the eagle flying high toward the sunlight of the spirit. Lifting higher and higher, you become a lighter and brighter version of yourself, no longer tethered to petty earthly concerns. Imagine you are so high now that which previously challenged you has fallen off your back, unable to breathe the purified air. Without so much as a backward glance, regal like the eagle, you need not spend your precious energy slumming with lower-level concerns, but rather creating your wish for the world.

MANTRA

My fearless spirit soars to the heights of my most awakened life.

Elephant

Be large and in charge.

Love will draw an elephant through a keyhole.
— SAMUEL RICHARDSON

ELEPHANT'S MESSAGE

Never forget how great and powerful you truly are! Take a moment to imagine that in one mighty stomp, all barriers and restrictions to the life of your dreams are suddenly flattened. Take a breath as you allow yourself to perceive your greatest, most abundant possibilities. By selecting the elephant card, you are reminded that nothing truly stands between you and your divine destiny — fortune, wealth, success, abundance, and fulfillment are yours now!

MEANING
When an elephant stomps or stampedes into your dream—or if it stands with its trunk lowered, inviting you to take a ride on its back—it tells you that whatever is troubling you is on its way out. This gentle giant reminds you that your loyalty has enormous power. You don't have to run around trying to prove that you are a big deal. Stand still, feel proud of your stature, and remember you stand upon the shoulders of giants. Make room for yourself to be recognized so that the blessings you've sought may fall at your feet.

MANIFESTATION
Make a list of the things you believe are standing in the way of your goal *du jour*. Envision becoming at one with Elephant as all obstacles become obsolete. Meditate on how good it feels to know you have the strength and wisdom to stomp out your fears and manifest your dreams.

MANTRA
I move with enormous confidence as there is room for the world within my heart.

Fish

Dive in! Prosperity is flowing.

*A fish only begins to realize its potential
the moment you throw it in deep waters.*
— MATSHONA DHLIWAYO

FISH'S MESSAGE
Are you a big fish in a small pond or a guppy surrounded by sharks? Have you been rigid? Could some practice playing scales improve your flexibility? How would you feel if you were truly in flow with your creative, sensual self? Perhaps you are like so many two-leggeds, with a schedule more crowded than a can of sardines. If this resonates, create more time for your feminine aspect to 'swim' — stretch out and explore your feelings. Empty

out, have a good cry. Then you can refill your tank with the creative energy that will truly feed your soul.

MEANING
Fish is considered a bringer of good luck and prosperity, courage and tenacity, depth and flow, intuition, and esoteric knowledge. Regardless of your gender or sexual orientation, dreams of fish are reminders of your fluidity. This waking or sleeping dream may connect you with your emotional, esoteric, spiritual, creative, sensual, and feeling side.

MANIFESTATION
Just as fish are likely to be unaware of the water all around them, your experience of financial lack may be a matter of perspective. Ask Fish to help you meditate in an ocean of material prosperity. Picture all your needs being met with waves of abundance. Carry this image with you throughout your day, and keep returning to the ocean of wealth within you.

MANTRA
I live in the slipstream of life, allowing all I seek to flow toward, through, and back to me.

Fox

Follow your cleverness.

Using trickery on the trickster to mend their ways is not trickery but the rightful use of intelligence.
— ABHIJIT NASKAR

FOX'S MESSAGE

Rules were made to be broken — especially if the rules are outmoded and in need of an update. It's okay to be cunning and sly when your intent is not just to meet your own needs but to benefit all, even if it's in a circuitous manner. Don't overthink. Swift action will help you find your way out of the box. It's time to contact the sacred by following the trail of humor and mischief that will take you there. And as an added benefit, the more you practice *blissipline* (discipline to access bliss), the more attractive (foxy) you become.

MEANING
Waking or sleeping dreams of Fox are a message to be flexible, nimble, creative, and quick on your feet, especially in the midst of a tricky situation. If you feel fenced in, call on Fox to help you access your wit, mental acuity, and grace that knows the most unconventional way to outsmart challenges.

MANIFESTATION
Since nighttime hours are best for hunting, call on Fox at bedtime to help you use your dreams to retrieve answers to a question or an insight you desire. Write down your question — then take a peek at it at bedtime. Upon awakening, journal any remembered scruff of a dream. Interpret your dream from the perspective that Fox delivers strange but relevant clues to help you become more alert, aware, and connected to your vital energy and good fortune.

MANTRA
As I embrace my inner trickster, I see that life is never happening to me but for me.

Frog

Don't worry, be hoppy.

If we can discover the meaning in the trilling of a frog, perhaps we may understand why it is for us not merely noise but a song of poetry and emotion.
— ADRIAN FORSYTH

FROG'S MESSAGE
Feeling swamped? Call on the power of your sacred tears to help cleanse away stagnant resentment, pain, and/or cynicism. When you are all cried out, take a leap of faith from the dankness of your earth-based reality all the way up to the realm of your sky-high dreams — and back again.

MEANING
When Frog hops into your sleeping or waking dream, consider yourself lucky. Frog is the ultimate alchemist. Their presence is a reminder to fall in love with your shadow side. When you embrace an aspect of life that you formerly shunned or relegated to your inner swamp, you don't transform *it*, but it transforms *you* into your warm-blooded, charming self. When we behold the beauty beneath our superficial warts and bestow the kiss of self-love—symbolic of embracing the unembraceable, loving the unlovable—we are transformed into royalty.

MANIFESTATION
Take some time out from the cacophony of trying to keep up with others, and instead, come to peace with your watery essence — take a bath, or go for a swim in a nearby pool, ocean, or lake. At least enjoy a tall drink of water to soothe a croaky throat. You'll catch more flies and dreams this way. Don't forget, I *toad* you so.

MANTRA
I leap from the lily pad of my comfort zone, over the obstacles, toward the new best version of me.

Giraffe

Hold your head high.

My interest in life comes from setting myself huge,
apparently unachievable challenges and trying to rise above them.
— RICHARD BRANSON

GIRAFFE'S MESSAGE

You were not given your stature to play small. All the camouflage in the world won't hide the fact that you have gifts, talents, and a perspective to share that sets you above the crowd — and it's time to own it. This is not about being arrogant — quite the opposite. In humble service, tune in to behold your bright future. Allow this inspiration to shine through you so that everyone in the jungle feels the glow of your vision and becomes moved to stick their neck out with you for a worthy cause.

MEANING
When you dream of a giraffe at night or see one by day, it is a blessing as it symbolizes you are connecting with your higher intelligence. This can help you glimpse the ultimate version of your future, along with the best, most beautiful path to get there. Giraffe reminds you to let your inner and outer beauty inspire others to rise above the fray and walk peacefully with grace — in this world, but not of it.

MANIFESTATION
To access your inner spiritual giant (aka Giraffe), take a deep breath, straighten your spine and move your awareness to the highest possible point of view you can find. Scientific research proves the effect of two-minute 'power poses' like this that can change your confidence level in the short and long term.

MANTRA
With my head held high and feet on the ground, I am a bridge between heaven and earth.

Goat

Trust yourself to climb high while remaining grounded.

*You just hold your head high and keep those fists down.
No matter what anybody says to you, don't you let 'em get your goat.
Try fightin' with your head for a change.*
— ATTICUS FINCH (HARPER LEE)

GOAT'S MESSAGE

Hold your ground on the issues you feel are most important. You may be called stubborn and headstrong, but only you can be the judge. It's true, not all battles are worth fighting — but it's good to know you can buck the system when required. Don't let anyone make you their scapegoat. As you climb toward the peak of your dreams, naysayers may try to get your goat. Just keep your eyes on the prize while holding fast to your navigational aptitude that will see you through the most treacherous mountain passes.

MEANING

In dreams, goats are symbolic of procreation, stubbornness, and financial abundance. Greek mythology associates goats with Dionysus, god of wine and pleasure, and Pan, who represents sexual hedonism, among other traits. In some Christian interpretations, goats are associated with being 'horny' and thus, devilish — which may explain why many people demonize pleasure. But this dream may encourage your determination as you pursue your pleasure principle — to claim it as a blessing for you, the world, and life itself.

MANIFESTATION

Contemplate a goal that feels just out of reach. Imagine the great joy you will feel when you arrive at the pinnacle moment of your quest. Let this wonderful feeling ripple down from the mountain peak to where you currently are to inspire you to keep climbing. Feel a rush of confidence, knowing your creator (God/Goddess/the Universe or who/whatever resonates for you) placed the pleasure of this goal in the center of your guidance system for a reason.

MANTRA

I keep my head down and charge forward toward my highest aspirations.

Gorilla

Take the lead as the gentle giant you are.

*The more you learn about the dignity of the gorilla,
the more you want to avoid people.*
— DIAN FOSSEY

GORILLA'S MESSAGE

It's time to realize the enormity of your impact on the people and environment around you. It's okay that until now, you've not been fully aware of the consequences of your choices, moods, and behaviors. But it's time for a reckoning. You rule, like a black belt martial artist, when you know the depths of your power. All remnants of prior insecurity, defensiveness, or ego-compensation are rendered unnecessary.

MEANING
Do you feel the need to shake the trees to get the attention you crave? Gorilla is here to tell you it's time to stop reacting to life like the underdog. In fact, consider that your days of 'not enoughness' and insecurity are over. When Gorilla enters your dream, it's a message to remember the potency of who you are.

MANIFESTATION
In order to stand tall in your nobility and uplevel your social interactions, allow Gorilla's gift for communication to empower you. Call to mind someone with whom you have an unresolved issue. Vent any anger, hurt, or disappointment you feel toward them in your journal—or in your car with the windows rolled up—before you address them. Primal scream and bang your chest if you have to. Once you've released the beast of your upset (in a way that doesn't hurt anyone), proceed with your actual communication calmly and effectively.

MANTRA
I'm aware of my impact, so I choose my words mindfully.

Horse

Jump over obstacles that fence you in.

I call horses 'divine mirrors' — they reflect back the emotions you put in. If you put in love and respect and kindness and curiosity, the horse will return that.
— ALLAN HAMILTON

HORSE'S MESSAGE
Have you been having a hard time saddling up to how amazing, capable, talented, and strong you are? It's time to unbridle your strength and indulge your appetite for freedom. This might bring you to a world beyond the corral of your comfort zone. Be attentive to what your soul says 'yes' to, and to what it says 'neigh'. You have the horsepower to leap over anything in the

way of actualizing your self-expression, beauty, and blazing sexual/sensual glory.

MEANING

Dreams of Horse come to those with a freedom-seeking soul. Associated with gentleness, intuition, independence, and travel, the horse likes to run wild while also enjoying the company of the herd. This dream may be nuzzling you so you'll stop looking gift horses in the mouth. Acknowledge those in your life who've carried you through circumstances you couldn't have traversed on your own. With Horse on your team, you will find a balance between independence and duty, harmony and self-expression. Just use your 'horse sense' (common sense) to discern when to attend to the team's needs and when to stride toward your most successful future.

MANIFESTATION

Horse represents success, but focus is required — and Horse naturally wants to take in the whole scene. So, when it comes to manifesting your goal, go ahead and put on your blinders for a few minutes as you give your undivided attention to doing the work it will take to make you feel accomplished. Once you've completed your goal, reward yourself by ripping off your blinders and taking some time to horse around (let yourself have some fun)!

MANTRA

I ride bareback through the prairie of my most passionate possibilities.

Hummingbird

Do your part with love.

Play well your part, therein the glory lies.
— WILLIAM SHAKESPEARE

HUMMINGBIRD'S MESSAGE

There is a story of a forest fire. All the animals flee for their lives except Hummingbird. Without wasting a moment, Hummingbird flies to a nearby stream, fills its beak, and soars over the forest fire releasing the water onto the fire. Back and forth it goes, while the other animals say, "Silly Hummingbird, you can't put out that fire with these drops of water. You're too small!" Hummingbird replies, "I'm just doing my part." This card is a reminder that while you can't do everything, you can do what is most important — that which is within your control. And sometimes, that can make all the difference.

MEANING
When you dream of Hummingbird, it reflects your ability to be still within productivity. Consider that a hummingbird's heart rate can beat 1,260 times per minute and flap its wings up to 70 times per second — all this while it appears to be standing still in midair. Hummingbird is a messenger, so feel into their communication for you — be playful, drink in the sweetness, raise your vibration, fly above the thorns, allow beauty to inspire you toward greater vitality, and may that vitality heal and inspire others.

MANIFESTATION
Resist the temptation to look around and determine your action based on what everyone else is doing or based on what your conditioning says you 'should' do. When you do what you are intrinsically wired and inspired to do, a sustainable, life-serving joy reverberates out and uplifts the birds of a feather who flock together with you.

MANTRA
I hum in rapturous vibration as I bring life-giving nectar to the world.

Insect

Honor the little things.

*Love has its own instinct, finding the way to the heart,
as the feeblest insect finds the way to its flower,
with a will which nothing can dismay nor turn aside.*
— HONORE DE BALZAC

INSECT'S MESSAGE

Have you been feeling underestimated or underutilized? Bugged by a stream of seemingly petty annoyances? Or maybe you've let the little things get under your skin. If so, consider the wise words of the late Richard Carlson, "Don't sweat the small stuff … and it's all small stuff." Also, consider that the angels—not the devils—are in the details. In other words, identifying and implementing the solution to your challenge can be easy once you are willing to behold and respect its most minute features. Your life might not need an entire overhaul, just a minuscule change that could make all the difference.

MEANING
Dreams of insects may tell you it takes a team to build a dream. Let Insect inspire you to be nimble as you adapt to your ever-changing circumstances. Insect's message is to be tenacious and remember that the part you play, though it may seem small, serves a larger role in the overall cosmic ecosystem.

MANIFESTATION
When you want to do big things but feel too small to make a difference, consider that life on Earth would perish if all insects disappeared. As Martin Rees says, "An insect is more complex than a star and is a far greater challenge to understand." Be persistent in your endeavors. Simply do what's in front of you, and one day you'll look back and see that you—and those you work with—have moved mountains. So, join with your community. If you don't yet have one, get out and find like-minded people who inspire you.

MANTRA
I'm buzzing with the power of communal support.

Monkey

Branch out, take a risk, and indulge your silly side.

*Stop waiting for fun to miraculously land at your feet.
Playfulness rewards the ones who go looking for it.*
— MEREDITH SINCLAIR

MONKEY'S MESSAGE
Playfulness is next to godliness. The telltale sign of your spiritual growth and enlightenment is your ability to swing freely from one vine of life to the next in whatever direction most delights your pleasure principle. Transform your monkey mind into the mind of a monk — the key is in your ability to let go of attachment to seriousness and find the divine humor in all of life … especially the parts that seem most dire. Remember —

tragedy plus time equals comedy.

MEANING
Monkey is known for being silly, finding *di-vine-ity* via playfulness. Nighttime dreams or daytime sightings of Monkey might be a message that it's time for you to expand your horizons by engaging your fun-loving child spirit. Conversely, it could symbolize that you've allowed the monkey mind to take over. Take heart in knowing your inner stillness can help you discern the difference between being childish or childlike, monkeying around and letting the monkeys run amok. The *monk-key* within you knows how to interweave playfulness and prayerfulness seamlessly throughout your day.

MANIFESTATION
Perhaps you've been seriously diligent upon your sacred path. And now, to uplevel your game, it's time to let loose. Instead of chastising, celebrate yourself when you make a mistake. You get extra points if you take time to goof off, laugh at yourself, and make a beautiful mess.

MANTRA
I am free to explore beyond my family tree. Should I fall, I know the whole jungle will catch me.

Mouse

Be nimble in adapting to life's changes.

*The quicker you let go of old cheese,
the sooner you find new cheese.*
— SPENCER JOHNSON

MOUSE'S MESSAGE

Have you been feeling restless and full of undirected hurry, scurry, worry, and flurry? Never fear, I'm here to ease your overwhelm — by encouraging you to hole up and try working solo for a while. While the rest of your pack hunts for cheese in all the traditional ways and places, your solo quest might lead you to unique ways of finding the loot you've been hungering for. Take time to become stealthy by burrowing into the unseen world, even if you have to don a coat of invisibility for a while. When you're ready to emerge into the light at the end of the tunnel, you'll pop your head out and be delighted at the wisdom (aka food for thought) you'll discover for yourself and to share with your pack.

MEANING

If you dream of Mouse, consider it a sign of wealth and success. Despite the bum rap mice get in many cultures, Mouse is mighty and comes bearing the strategy of survival—to help you in business or relationships—via resilient resourcefulness, especially during times of challenge. Just remember — if you've been feeling trapped in a corner, regardless of your size, stature, or place in the world, when you take care of the little things that are under your control, one day you'll discover they'll add up to making a big difference.

MANIFESTATION

Because Mouse is connected to the earth element, it is here to help you become more grounded. Take an exit ramp off the rat race, if even for only a day, hour, or minute. Simply turn off your phone or computer, sit on the ground, walk barefoot in nature, or tend to your garden. These simple acts—that, like Mouse, are so easily overlooked—can go a long way toward infusing you with mightiness.

MANTRA

I can do great things in this life, one teeny-tiny step at a time.

Octopus

Be flexible.

*What she taught me was to feel ...
that you're part of this place, not a visitor.
That's a huge difference.*
— CRAIG FOSTER

OCTOPUS' MESSAGE

Are you in the midst of an important time in your life? If so, you've chosen this card to bring your inner MacGyver (aka Octopus) to the forefront — your innovator who never laments a lack of resources. Octopus knows that everything you need is everything you have. Most people resist change, but you have what it takes to embrace it successfully. Use your head and remember the infinite possibilities surrounding you in the ocean of emotion. Pulling this card means you are more equipped than you realize to excel in your current circumstance. As a natural caregiver, remember that compassion isn't compassion unless there's some left for you. In other words, you're no one's sucker. Just take time for regeneration and renewal—especially when you feel sucked dry—and you'll always have a full tank from which to enrich others.

MEANING

Dreams of Octopus are a message to tap into your *in-eight* talents to better handle the changing tides you are swimming through. In addition to symbolizing infinity (due to their eight limbs), versatility, dexterity, intelligence, and enlightened consciousness, Octopus reminds you to metamorphosize, so you may better serve those around you — because as you are lifted with the rising tide, all are lifted.

MANIFESTATION

It's time to take stock of your myriad gifts, resources, and special skills. Are you creative, passionate, sensitive, smart, and hardworking? Counting your charms (aka keeping track of all the blessings in your amazing life, internal and external) will give you the confidence to adapt, flow, and find your way to your inner treasure chest.

MANTRA

With eight-fold blessings on my side, I have all I need to adapt to the changing seas.

Owl

See beyond the obvious.

I like the night. Without the dark, we'd never see the stars.
— STEPHENIE MEYER

OWL'S MESSAGE

You have extrasensory power and perception. Do not be frightened of it. And do not fear the dark — it's where the most incredible gifts tiptoe out of hiding and reveal themselves. Open your inner and outer eyes to behold the greatest secrets never told. Once you acclimate, you'll discover night vision that enables you to see what escapes most people.

MEANING
Nighttime dreams or daytime sightings of Owl symbolize that you are coming into your wisdom, magic, and ability to see in the dark — beyond the limitations of the conscious mind. Owl reminds you that your shadow and the unknown are your friends. Access your inner owl when acclimating to a new nest, town, project, or relationship. Owl is also known for being a protector. When they show up in dreams, it's as if they are giving you another set of eyes—in the back of your head—to bring you a 360-degree view of the terrain you are navigating.

MANIFESTATION
In Greek mythology, Owl is the animal companion of the goddess Athena — known for her seriousness, intelligence, ability to focus and to swoop in and get needs met on behalf of herself and her people. With Owl—and Athena—in mind, in the quiet of night, when the world is asleep, and there are no distractions, call to mind a goal, wish, or desire you would most love to *dream-a-fest* (manifest, using the help of your dreaming mind). Imagine you are at one with Owl, beholding with laser focus the jewel in the midst of your desire. Allow Owl's steady gaze to guide you toward fulfilling your intent.

MANTRA
The mystery of the darkness is my friend. I have a HOOT getting my most essential needs met.

Peacock

Remember you are special … just like everyone else.

I shall always remember how the peacocks' tails shimmered when the moon rose amongst the tall trees, and on the shady bank, the emerging mermaids gleamed fresh and silvery amongst the rocks …
— HERMANN HESSE

PEACOCK'S MESSAGE

The time has come to recognize and own your beauty — inside and out. This is not about becoming egotistical. It's humble to realize you are a gift to this planet. When you know your true power comes from the Divine, you'll find it easier to shine. With this in mind, don't hide your gorgeousness under a bushel. It's time to bring forth your best and brightest in the boardroom, bedroom, and everywhere you grace. If you've got it—which you do—flaunt it, and uplift all of life.

MEANING

Have you been trying to prove your worth to others? Dreams of Peacock are to help you behold your royal stature and the humility to maintain balance and be approachable. It's believed that peacocks' plumes are so brilliant because of the thorns they eat, which make them the ultimate symbol of alchemy. If you dream of Peacock, let this be a message to metabolize past traumas or present challenges and transform them into vivid plumage in the form of great compassion and wisdom. When a peacock molts, its feathers grow back to their original grandeur. As such, peacocks symbolize resurrection and enlightenment and teach us how the proper use of color can evoke magic.

MANIFESTATION

It's time to re-evaluate your beliefs about beauty, pride, and full-throttle self-expression. Grab your journal and unfurl your beliefs and prejudices about flamboyance. Does it fascinate you? Do you hate it? Judge it? Does it scare or intimidate you? With great power comes greater responsibility. So, with Peacock as your ally, explore healthy self-esteem by shining the rainbow of your inner light today. Wear something bright and present yourself as if you were ready for showtime.

MANTRA

I shake my tail feather. As I strut my true colors, I invite others to do the same.

Pig

You've got plenty, so share the wealth.

The world is mud-luscious and puddle-wonderful.
— E. E. CUMMINGS

PIG'S MESSAGE

Have you been grappling with whether or not to take the big piece of the pie? As long as you dedicate your good fortune to allowing others to live high on the hog too, then go ahead and chow down to your heart's content. But if you've been taking more than you've been giving, perhaps this is a message to lift your gaze, look around, and share your abundance.

MEANING
If you dream of Pig, consider it a sign of good luck and prosperity. Pig is the ultimate symbol of bounty, which is why people use piggy banks for savings. Pig's ego does not yearn for the limelight, and they're not penned in by caring what others think. With this in mind, refrain from pandering to others' egos, contorting to meet their needs, or worrying about whether or not they recognize how smart, wonderful, and beautiful you are. With Pig on your side, you can root forward, under the radar of those who might turn their nose up at you, toward the life that will make you happier than a pig in mud.

MANIFESTATION
Do you feel unappreciated or unrecognized? If so, come clean about it in your journal. Give yourself time—a few minutes, maybe even a day—to wallow in the mire of self-pity. When you are complete, take a long, hot shower or bath. Wash the person or situation out of your hair. Resolve to no longer cast your pearls (wisdom, talent, or love) before an undeserving audience. Save your pearls for those who are genuinely worthy of your specialness.

MANTRA
No matter the mud I fall into, I always emerge exfoliated.

Rabbit

Be your own good luck charm.

There are many talented people who haven't fulfilled their dreams because they overthought it, or they were too cautious and were unwilling to make the leap of faith.
— JAMES CAMERON

RABBIT'S MESSAGE

Do you want more abundance in your life? Is there a miracle you're trying to pull out of your hat? Is it time to implement a plan, and you are unsure if you should zig or you should zag? If so, today's your lucky day. Hop to it! Trust your 'wild hare' instincts and use your intelligence to manifest what you need, even if it seems like magical thinking — too good to be true. You drew this card as a message to alchemize your fears so you can more powerfully manifest your dreams in the world. When you are ready, leap into the unknown.

MEANING
Dreams of Rabbit tell you it's time to stop, drop, look, and listen like never before. Because Rabbit is the symbol of fertility, abundance, and good luck, this dream might portend a grand-scale win — meeting your soul mate, or discovering you are pregnant with a baby, or a life-changing creative idea. Either way, prepare yourself. Good things are multiplying for you.

MANIFESTATION
Call on Rabbit when you're feeling stuck in a rut or thinking you must plan and control every detail. An expert at burrowing underground, myths and legends consider Rabbit a shamanic guide between heaven, earth, and the underworld. Rabbit invites you to dig past the topsoil of collective understanding to the deeper truth of your area of expertise — venture down a path of fascination, or throw yourself into a passion project. As you journey beyond the outer reaches of your psyche, prepare to encounter the bizarre or unusual like Alice did when she followed the White Rabbit. The good fortune you discover might just blow your mind.

MANTRA
I keep my wits about me as I venture down the rabbit hole of lucky opportunities.

Shark

Be fierce.

Avoiding danger is no safer in the long run than outright exposure. The fearful are caught as often as the bold.
— HELEN KELLER

SHARK'S MESSAGE

Do you suppress your anger because you're afraid that if you unleash it, you might bite someone's head off? Or do you fear you might be encircled by unsavory people who will try to drag you down? If so, I'm here to protect you and help you adapt to challenging circumstances. This card encourages you to delve into the deep waters of your greatest dreams. With me swimming beside you, you can let your faith become bigger than your fear.

MEANING
When Shark swims into your awareness, it might be a message to get a grip on your aggressive emotions, or to protect yourself if you're swimming in tumultuous waters that are over your head. Even though sharks are thought of as the 'predators' of the sea, their association with water invites you to consider that your 'adversaries' may be more sensitive than you think. Or perhaps you need to be more shark-like in your life, allowing the intensity of your inward drive to move you forward. Ultimately, because Shark cannot stop swimming, the message here may be not to stop — keep moving with the current of life, and you will find your way.

MANIFESTATION
You may have heard the saying, 'Everything you want is on the other side of fear'. In that spirit, do something today that scares you — even if it's in the privacy of your journal. Circle around your desire and imagine plunging in. *Fin* for yourself (gather what you need) until you emerge unapologetically victorious.

MANTRA
I stay sharp and move forward toward my dreams.

Skunk

Don't make a stink … unless absolutely necessary.

Smell is the closest thing human beings have to a time machine.
— CARYL RIVERS

SKUNK'S MESSAGE
Have people accused you of being overly dramatic, but you know you're a pacifist at heart? Perhaps they misunderstand that the 'stink eye' you give is simply a warning. You know, if you really wanted to, you could wreak havoc when provoked. But perhaps you've chosen this card to remind yourself to only charge into battle if absolutely necessary — once you've exhausted all other options. To prevent getting to this point, call on me to help you set firm boundaries with people in your life.

MEANING
Dreams of Skunk are a message to pay attention to your *instinks*. Because skunks keep their predators at bay by spraying a foul stench, this dream begs the question — have you been putting up a smoke screen to keep intimacy away? If this is the case, explore how healthy communication might help you feel safe to love. It takes skunks up to ten days to refill their scent glands — their message is to pick your battles. Only unleash your defense mechanisms when you genuinely need to, so you're not left depleted. Alternatively, because skunks are black and white, ask yourself if you've fallen prey to black and white (stinking) thinking.

MANIFESTATION
Do you feel like a wallflower or a cog in the wheel at work? Skunk is here to help you dig down deep in the soil of your soul to discover your unique style (signature scent). Take a few moments to call to mind—or write in your journal—the qualities that make you stand out. If you're having a hard time with this, interview a few close loved ones to share what they feel is most special about you. Take these reflections with you, raise your tail, and parade about with the confidence you deserve.

MANTRA
I sniff out the truth, then set exquisite boundaries.

Snake

Behold your ssssacred ssssensuality.

I take pleasure in my transformations. I look quiet and consistent, but few know how many women there are in me.
— ANAÏS NIN

SNAKE'S MESSAGE
It's time to shed attachments to identities that no longer serve you so that you can reinvent yourself anew. Drop rigidity, and let yourself flow with boneless fluidity while discerning who you let into your heart. In other words, make sure people are worthy before granting them access to the intimacy of your ssssacred garden.

MEANING
Snake slithering through your night dream or daydream symbolizes renewal and healing, as it was in many ancient Greek traditions. Snake's not just a phallic symbol — thank you, Sigmund Freud. Because they shed their skin, snakes represent being able to start over, reset, and return to innocence, no matter what's happened in your past. Because many people are afraid of snakes, they can be perceived as a warning to be wary of seduction by a silver-tongued someone. However, some ancient teachings suggest that a snake represents wisdom earned by facing and embracing your shadow.

MANIFESTATION
Ask yourself, "What area of my life, heart, or body is most in need of healing now?" In a meditative state, envision this area receiving the antivenom/medicine it needs as you shed the skin of past pain. Allow yourself to imagine the healing being granted and integrated, so much so that your issue no longer exists — *voila!* Now ask yourself, "What will I do/manifest/create with all this new, available energy?"

MANTRA
I celebrate the soul medicine that comes from my irresisssssstible power to transform!

Spider

Weave your best dreams into reality.

… Life is interrelated. All men are caught in an inescapable network of mutuality, tied in a single garment of destiny … I can never be what I ought to be until you are what you ought to be, and you can never be what you ought to be until I am what I ought to be …
— MARTIN LUTHER KING JR.

SPIDER'S MESSAGE

Have you been feeling trapped or stuck in a creative rut? Remember, *you* are the weaver of your destiny. You can unravel even the most challenging pattern and rework it to your advantage. You've pulled this card to remind yourself that you are intrinsically woven into the divine plan, and your higher self is luring you toward your most exalted purpose.

MEANING
Regardless of what you may think, a day or nighttime visit from Spider is a good omen, steeped in magic and empowerment. Spider symbolizes communication, creativity, and innovation — so is it any wonder that most of us spend our days inexorably connected to the 'World Wide Web'? Spider in a dream is helping you tap into your inner strategist—or seductress—to weave your greatest desires into reality. Follow your dreams — rather than, say, step on them or swat them with a broom. Spiders attract what they need, and are often associated with the divine feminine.

MANIFESTATION
Most people say they want more love, magic, and miracles in their life. Yet, Spider medicine tells us there is no lack of what we desire. The things we most deeply want exist in multitudes. With this in mind, instead of cajoling life for what you want, make the space for your desires to be drawn to you. Take a few minutes to create breathing room in your calendar. Clear your counters, nightstand, and closets of clutter, and make your living or workspace appealing. Now allow life to bring what you need to your doorstep.

MANTRA
I stay connected to the gossamer threads that bind me to my highest destiny.

Squirrel

**Prepare for the future
while playfully enjoying the present.**

*Millions of trees in the world are accidentally planted by squirrels —
who bury nuts, then forget where they hid them.
Do good and forget. It'll grow someday.*
— ANONYMOUS

SQUIRREL'S MESSAGE

Do you need some motivation to move toward your goals, as nutty as they may seem? Have your best-laid plans ground to a halt? Or are you feeling like you are up a tree and out on a limb? If so, Squirrel's here to infuse you with comedy and joy to reanimate your lighthearted spirit. Once you're back to your vibrant self, get ready to romp.

MEANING

If Squirrel skitters across your waking or sleeping dream, consider this a sign of good news, positivity, and abundance — be it in your resources, money, or playfulness. Squirrel in a dream may also be a message to be practical with your providence — in other words, ration and spend conservatively to make your abundance last — or better yet, compound with interest! This is not to say hoard, become miserly, or cling overly to material goods. As long as you have what you need, you'll be content.

MANIFESTATION

Squirrel says there's no time like the present to care for your future self. Do you need a life insurance policy or an update to your will? Tackle the toughest action items on your list — the phone call you resist, the chore you cringe at, the confrontation that makes your heart palpitate. In other words, burrow in and work during your productive seasons—spring and summer— so you can feast on your reserves come fall and winter … just make sure to keep track of where you stash your loot!

MANTRA

I'm nuts about my job! I love what I do and do what I love.

Tortoise

Make progress, one step at a time.

*To the man who can perfectly practice inaction,
all things are possible.*
—ERNEST HOLMES

TORTOISE'S MESSAGE

Does life feel topsy-turvy? Does it seem that the *hurrier* you go the *behinder* you get? Or are major changes flipping your world upside down? If so, Tortoise is here to help you get back on your feet, on your true path, at your true pace. You've chosen this card as a reminder that you are loved and lovable just as you are. Slow down and smell (and maybe even nibble on) the roses. Consider that from the highest perspective, there is no need to hurry. Wherever you go, there you are — and that's where the party is!

MEANING

Being one of the oldest animals to walk the earth, Tortoise is the ultimate symbol for long life, endurance, and strength. When Tortoise ambles into your dream, it may be a message to slow down. Your inner stillness is the key to overcoming your obstacles. Connected to Tortoise, no one can rush you into the fray until or unless you are ready. Yet when it's time for action, change, or even a wanderlust walk-about, you can do so with confidence, knowing you carry home with you, wherever you roam. And when you feel ready to get naked (emotionally or otherwise), you'll emerge from the sanctuary of your shell, powerful in your vulnerability, cloaked energetically with your connection to Spirit and the ancient ones who walk with you.

MANIFESTATION

In order to behold life's greatest miracles that reside right in front of you, take a slow, tortoise-like, meditative walk. Exhale as you imagine letting go of the weight of the world you've been carrying on your back. Release any tension from your shoulders as you inhale serene power from the center of Mother Earth. Walk gently, and know that with each step, Tortoise is transforming you into the one-of-a-kind, self-actualized, spiritual being you incarnated to be.

MANTRA

I pace myself, knowing life is a marathon, not a sprint, and I'm right where I'm supposed to be.

Unicorn

Reveal your true sparkle.

*When someone told me that I live in a fantasy land,
I nearly fell off my unicorn.*
— UNKNOWN

UNICORN'S MESSAGE

Let go of doubts and worries—even responsibilities—for a while. Suspend all disbelief and know you are loved by the divine spirits you can see and the ones you can't. You are unique and amazing, so let your sparkle show everywhere you go! If you've been suppressing your creative pursuits, pulling this card is the message to take a U-turn and get back on that horse (so to speak). With a beginner's mind, charge forth into the enchanted forest of your soul to reclaim the magic you once knew was real.

MEANING

Could there be a greater omen of good luck than the presence of Unicorn in a (waking or sleeping) dream? Probably not. When sparkly, glittery Unicorn trots into your dream, it's a sign of magic, happiness, and of wishes coming true. Unicorn dreams are also associated with financial abundance, purity, freedom, joy, and innocence. If you've been praying for a sign, consider this it. This may be a message to reengage with your creativity or to take it to a higher—or deeper—level. Because it's believed Unicorn only appears to the pure of heart, consider this card an affirmation that your spiritual/enlightenment work is paying off.

MANIFESTATION

To attract Unicorn into your realm, declutter your space and fill it with crystals and vibrant rainbow colors. Imagine that Unicorn is with you, granting your wish. Feel the wonder of your greatest desire coming true. Imagine taking a ride on Unicorn's back, syncing your vibration to its sky-high wavelength. As you ride, know you are partnering with Unicorn in raising consciousness on the planet — one person at a time, one dream at a time, and one unicorn sighting at a time.

MANTRA

I embrace unicorn magic in my life and watch as my dream world becomes actualized.

Whale

Behold your largesse.

*You can either see yourself as a wave in the ocean,
or you can see yourself as the ocean.*
— OPRAH WINFREY

WHALE'S MESSAGE
You are being invited to explore the deep end of your soul. Whale is beckoning you to say 'yes' to your most bountiful, enlightened potential. Because whales are believed to be of a higher consciousness than humans—some even think they come from another galaxy—by entraining to Whale's wavelength, your awakening is heightened, deepened, quickened, and expanded throughout the entire ocean of life.

MEANING
Nighttime dreams or daytime sightings of whales symbolize that you are connecting with your oceanic intelligence, wisdom, and power. This dream may help you remember that in any circumstance, *your charge is to enlarge*. In other words, let your heart grow as big and deep as the ocean. As you do this, you will discover abundant solutions and resources that make life no longer a problem to solve but pure *ecsta-sea* to explore.

MANIFESTATION
When you face a challenge, imagine dropping to the deep end of your inner ocean, where there is always calm. Breathe in sync with your inner whale, allowing its oceanic wisdom to support your every move. Imagine the waves splashing over you, purifying you of any barnacles from the shallow end. Now visualize riding your wisdom to the ocean's surface, spraying Whale's healing effects on the world.

MANTRA
Through the ups and downs of my emotional waves, I have a whale of a time.

Wolf

Indulge your soul's hunger.

If believing in yourself and going after what you want in life and realizing your worth is ruthless and selfish, then I'm definitely ruthless and selfish.
— NICOLE SCHERZINGER

WOLF'S MESSAGE

Have you been biting back your true feelings? Have you been torn between the call of the wild telling you it's time to roam and your desire for domestic stability? If so, Wolf is here to reflect that you can have both freedom and connection. Your intuition knows what your soul needs and can guide you on the higher path to a successful win/win/win situation.

MEANING

When Wolf prowls into your dream, it is a message to embrace your untamed power as you go after what you are truly hungering for. Wolf symbolizes wildness, loyalty, perseverance, and successful partnerships. This card may be a message that your pack is coming to claim you—if they haven't already—to initiate you into their clan. A clan who understands that in addition to the closeness of community, you also need your own (lone wolf) time in sacred solitude.

MANIFESTATION

Create agreements and boundaries with your partner and/or pack, so that when you need alone time, you get it. Be willing to take a road trip, solo excursion into nature, or an evening at home alone to stoke the flame of your independence. If you are the loner type, dare to venture to a public venue, where like-minded pack mates gather to celebrate a shared interest.

MANTRA

I howl at the full moon in full throttle self-expression of my wild heart and soul.

About the Author

KELLY SULLIVAN WALDEN is on a mission to awaken the world to the power of dreams. Known as Doctor Dream, Kelly is an award-winning bestselling author of books, oracle decks and meditations. Her latest book is *A Crisis is a Terrible Thing to Waste: The Art of Transforming the Tragic into Magic* (named Woman's World Book of the Week and in *Aspire Magazine's* Top 10 Most Inspirational books). Kelly is a dream expert, certified clinical hypnotherapist, inspirational speaker, and workshop facilitator who holds a doctorate degree in interfaith studies. Her unique approach to dream work has led her to consult with thousands of individuals from Fortune 500 executives to celebrities to stay-at-home moms. She's had the honor of interpreting dreams for Doctor Oz, Ricki Lake, George Noory (Coast to Coast) the hosts from The Real, Topher Grace, the Housewives of NY and many more. She hosts *The Kelly Sullivan Walden Show* podcast and is the founder of DreamWork

Practitioner Training (**www.KellySullivanWalden.com/ DreamWork**), an online professional-development program empowering people to incorporate dream work into their careers. To invite her to speak at your next event, for media inquiries, to receive your free JETSET dream interpretation worksheet (and/or to find out if the rumors that she's the love-grandchild of Carl Jung and Lucille Ball are true) visit **www.KellySullivanWalden.com** or connect with Kelly at:

Facebook: **KellySullivanWaldenDreams**
TikTok: **KellySullivanWald**
Twitter and Instagram: **KellySWalden**
YouTube: **www.youtube.com/@KellySullivanWalden**

Kelly is the author of *The Hero's Journey Dream Oracle, Dream Oracle Cards, Dream Goddess Empowerment Deck, Awakened Dreamer Oracle Cards, Luminous Humanness Oracle Cards* and *Dia de los Muertos Oracle.* Her books include I *Had the Strangest Dream, It's All in Your Dreams, Dreaming Heaven, The Love, Sex & Relationship Dream Dictionary, Chicken Soup for the Soul: Dreams and Premonitions, Chicken Soup for the Soul: Dreams and the Unexplainable,* and *Luminous Humanness.* Her other creations include *The Hero's Journey Dream Meditations* and *The Hero's Journey Dream Journal.*

About the Artist

LISA DESIMINI started drawing and painting as a young child and never stopped. When she grew up, she received a BFA from The School of Visual Arts in NYC where she later taught illustration for several years.

Lisa is an award-winning illustrator of over thirty-five books for children. Some of those books she has written herself. Her work has also graced the covers of many book jackets, including *The Sookie Stackhouse Series* by Charlaine Harris (which was turned into HBO's *True Blood*). Recently she was commissioned to illustrate a special edition of *The Man Who Fell to Earth*, released in fall 2022.

Lisa is known for exploring new mediums. She has worked with oils, acrylics, collage, photography, and sculpture. Sometimes she combines all of these techniques on the computer. No matter what the medium, Lisa's work is infused with a magical, otherworldly quality that speaks to all ages.

She lives with her husband and two cats in Los Angeles.

You can see more of Lisa's work at: **www.lisadesimini.com**

Also available from Blue Angel Publishing®

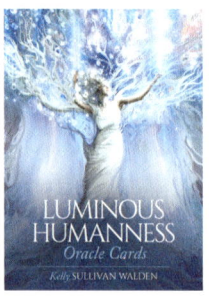

LUMINOUS HUMANNESS ORACLE CARDS

KELLY SULLIVAN WALDEN
Artwork by Laila Savolainen

To be luminous is to be at ease with your inner gold. In feeling and freeing your authentic, connected, and whole self, your light illuminates your path and possibilities so you can move forward in confidence and clarity, excited for all that awaits you.

Bestselling author Kelly Sullivan Walden rolls insight, imagination, and joy into this gorgeous oracle, elevating perspective and turning everyday tedium into treasured moments and glowing experiences.

44 Cards & 116-Page Guidebook
ISBN: 978-1-922573-69-8

Also available from Blue Angel Publishing®

DREAM GODDESS EMPOWERMENT DECK

KELLY SULLIVAN WALDEN

They may be hidden, but wisdom, empowerment, sensuality and creativity are inherent in everyone. The Goddesses are here to encourage you forward, to show you the wonders you are capable of, to reveal your innate strengths, intuition and compassion, and to remind you of the many resources you have within.

Bestselling author Kelly Sullivan Walden helps you view the world through goddess lenses with 55 inspiring messages to maximize your blessings and actualize love, health, abundance and fulfillment in your modern life. Connect with the wise and eternal Goddesses for greater awareness, life-enhancing magic and soul-enriching freedom.

55 Message Cards Plus Instruction Card
ISBN: 978-1-925538-80-9

Also available from Blue Angel Publishing®

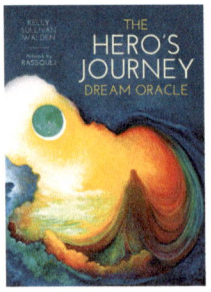

THE HERO'S JOURNEY DREAM ORACLE

KELLY SULLIVAN WALDEN
Artwork by Rassouli

Since time immemorial, the hero's journey has been taken by wizards, goddesses, sages, and ordinary people, and whether you realize or not, you are taking it right now. You have been called from your everyday world, to quest for change, for knowledge, for peace, for strength. You may have already crossed the threshold, discovered treasure, or be on the way home, changed, empowered and ready to share your wisdom. Wherever you are in your journey, the 52 cards of this unique deck are your willing, supportive and trustworthy companions.

Awaken the hero within, unlock the hidden insights of your dreams, and navigate every stage of your quest, with *The Hero's Journey Dream Oracle.*

52 Cards & 152-Page Guidebook
ISBN: 978-1-925538-48-9

Also available from Blue Angel Publishing®

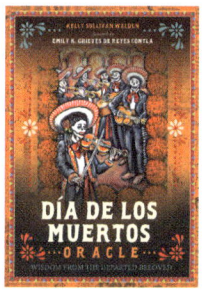

DÍA DE LOS MUERTOS ORACLE
Wisdom from the Departed Beloved

KELLY SULLIVAN WALDEN
Artwork by Emily K. Grieves de Reyes Contla

Painted in Teotihuacán, México, the vivid imagery of this oracle offers a wealth of symbolism alongside inspirational messages and practices for honoring and communing with your ancestors. Shuffle the deck, choose a card, and welcome angels, saints, memories, music, meaning, and spirit into your heart, home, readings, and meditations. Weave possibility, support, and purpose throughout your world with the mystical threads of Día de los Muertos.

44 Cards & 216-Page Guidebook
ISBN: 978-1-922573-52-0

For more information on this
or any Blue Angel Publishing® release,
please visit our website at:

www.blueangelonline.com